OXFORD ANTHEMS

General Editor David Willcocks

A 451
SATB (with divisions) unaccompanied

Joy is come!

Andrew Carter

MUSIC DEPARTMENT

OXFORD
UNIVERSITY PRESS

Joy is come!

Words by Andrew Carter

Tune: German 1360
arranged by
ANDREW CARTER

Printed in Great Britain

OXFORD UNIVERSITY PRESS, MUSIC DEPARTMENT, GREAT CLARENDON STREET, OXFORD OX2 6DP

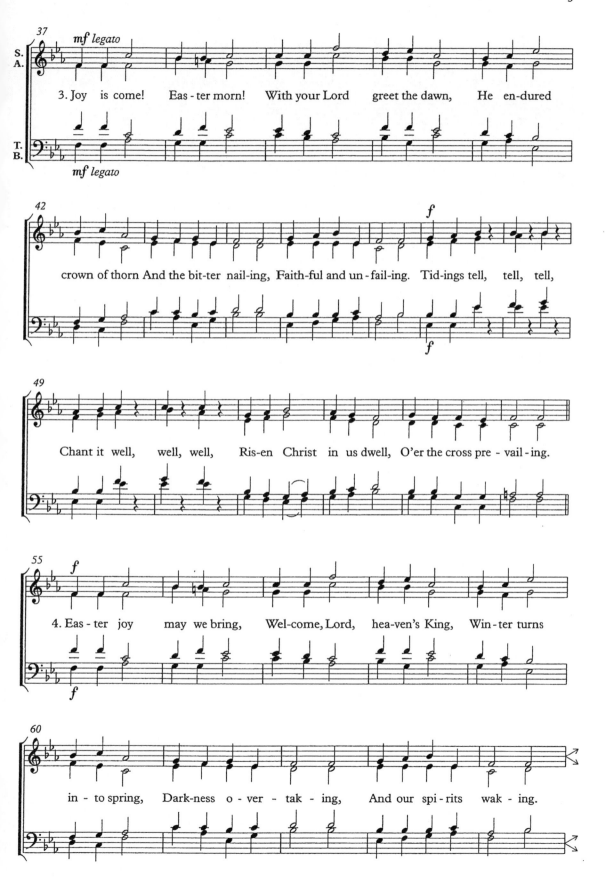

ISBN 978-0-19-350506-3

Music origination by Barnes Music Engraving Ltd., East Sussex.
Printed by Halstan & Co. Ltd., Aylesbury, Bucks., England.

9 780193 505063